The Making of
The Star of Texas

Written by Joseph E. Kasson
Illustrated by Lucas Adams

Kasson Publishing   Austin, Texas

The Making of The Star of Texas

Written by Joseph E. Kasson
Illustrated by Lucas Adams

Inquiries should be addressed to:
Kasson Publishing
201 E. St. Elmo Rd.
Austin, Texas 78745
e-mail   publishing@kassonscastings.com
www.kassonscastings.com

First Edition

ISBN: 0-9729435-8-7
Library of Congress Catalog Card Number: 2003091348

Acknowledgements

"The Making of the Star of Texas" is an independent publication and was not commissioned by the Bob Bullock Texas State History Museum. The Kasson family would like to acknowledge the following people without whom the Bronze Star of Texas could not have been possible:

*Bob Bullock- whose idea it was to build the museum and who guided the museum project through the Legislature.

*Angela and Mort Topfer of Austin- who donated the funds for the star.

*Earl Broussard of TBG Partners, Austin- who designed the star.

When I was a little boy, my brother and sister and I used to help my daddy and grandpa at work. We did all kinds of projects together! Ever since I can remember, we had always been a big help to my dad and grandpa in our foundry. At the foundry we melt bronze ingots that look like bricks made of bronze. We then pour the hot liquid bronze into special ceramic molds. Inside of these molds are the shapes of the bronze statues that we make.

Over the years we have made many different kinds of animals, both big and small. We have made elephants, orangutans, turtles, Komodo dragons, gorillas, manatees, birds, horses, longhorns, and the list goes on and on. We have also made statues of people--some of these statues are in the Texas State Capitol Building here in Austin. Once, we made a giant bronze mammoth that stands in front of the Dallas Museum of Natural History in Dallas, Texas.

When I was in school, I always had fun, but I had even more fun working in our shop after school and on weekends. Since I am bigger and older now, I am able to be a lot more help to my dad and grandpa, so now I work on projects that are really, really big. Now, I want to tell you about the moumental bronze star that we made. It stands in front of the Bob Bullock Texas State History Museum in Austin, Texas!

The first step in making the star was to plan out every detail very carefully. We had to think really hard about the best way to do our work. We also had to think about all the materials we would need and where to get those materials.

I was surprised at how much time we spent planning for the building of the star. I was ready to go to work on it right away, but my dad said it was best to spend more time in the planning stages so that once we began to work, everything would go smoother and easier for us. As the time came closer for us to actually begin our work on the star, our excitement grew and grew! One of the first things we did was write down a schedule showing the kind of work and how much we would have to do each day in order to have the star finished on time. Then, each morning while we ate breakfast together, we talked about our plans for the day and about how much work we had to complete before we could stop for the day. We began our work each morning while it was still dark outside.

One of the first things that we needed to do was to re-arrange our shop so that we would have lots of room to work on such a big project. It was a good thing we made all that room, because we needed every inch of space we could get.

Because the star was going to be so big, we had to do most of our work outside. We knew we would be using big cranes, boom lifts and forklifts, and none of these would fit inside our shop.

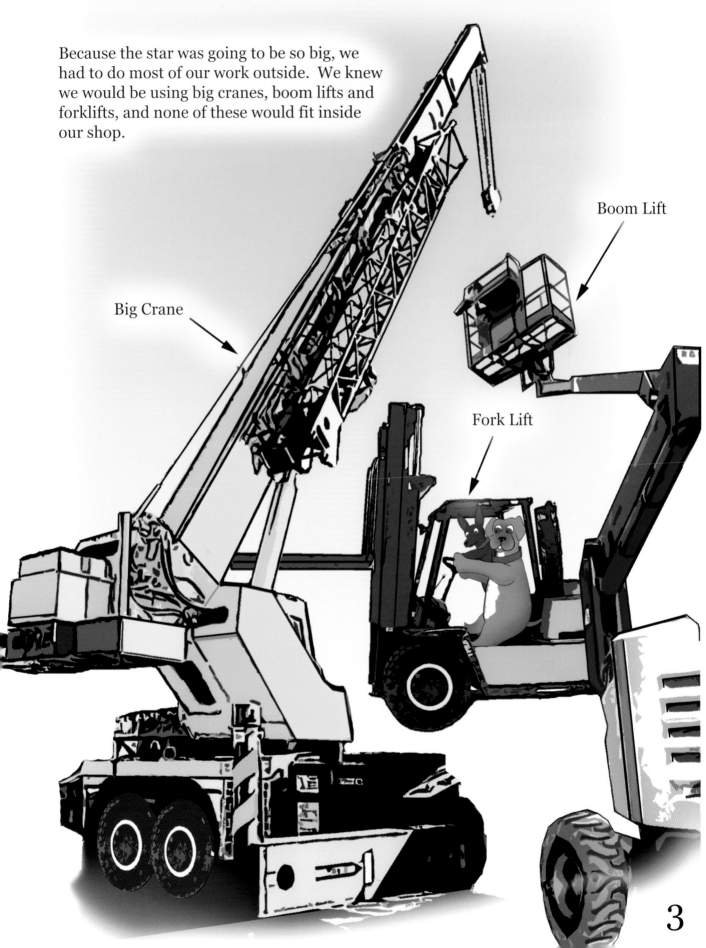

Boom Lift

Big Crane

Fork Lift

3

We are the real dogs, I'm Papa...

...and I'm Doyle.

Do you think they'll feed us more if it looks like we're working?

Of course!

Before we started building the giant star, we had a nice grassy area with flowers and plants in front of our foundry. Sometimes for lunch, we would have picnics there! However, since we needed all the space we could get, we put a fence up around that area so that we could use it for stacking materials and storing parts and pieces of the giant star.

This gave our two dogs, Doyle and Papa, a new area to explore and watch over. They think it's their job to always be on guard so that they can let us know whenever we have company or whenever there is a squirrel in the yard! Most of the time Papa sleeps while Doyle does the patrolling. Whenever Doyle discovers something while on patrol, he tells Papa, and Papa checks it out. If Papa decides it's worth telling us about, then they both start barking while they spin in circles.

4

Up until this time, we stayed very busy doing all the necessary preparation work. Finally, the big day came for us to start welding. We knew that we would first need to make 20 large triangles. These 20 triangles would all be the same shape and the same size – about 20 feet long and 6 feet tall.

To make the star, we needed to make…

20 large triangles   so that we could make
10 half cones   so that we could make
5 full cones   so that we could make

1   GIANT STAR

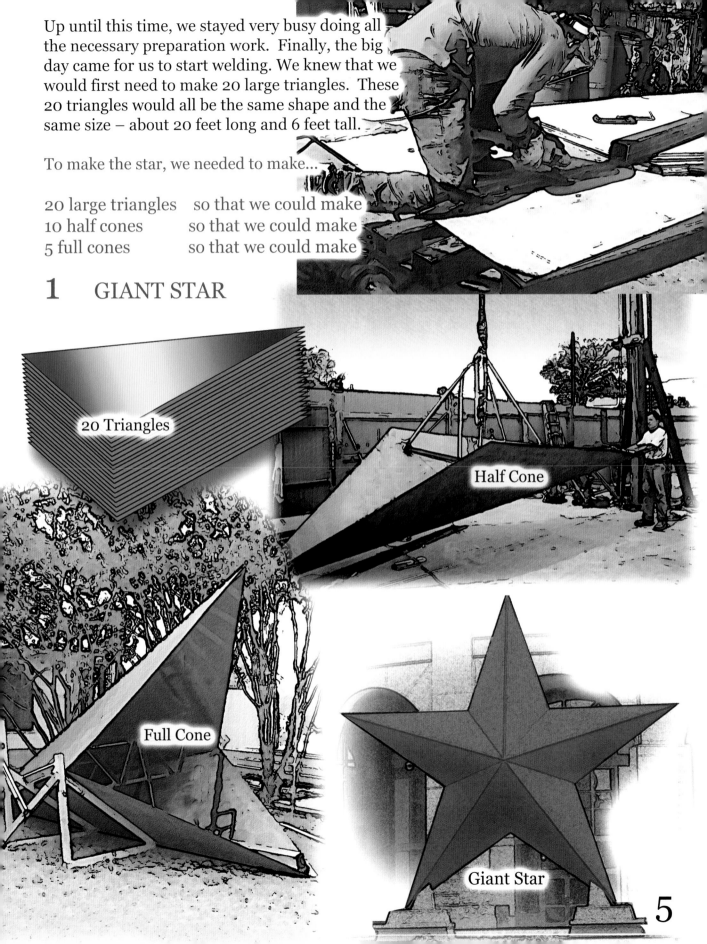

20 Triangles

Half Cone

Full Cone

Giant Star

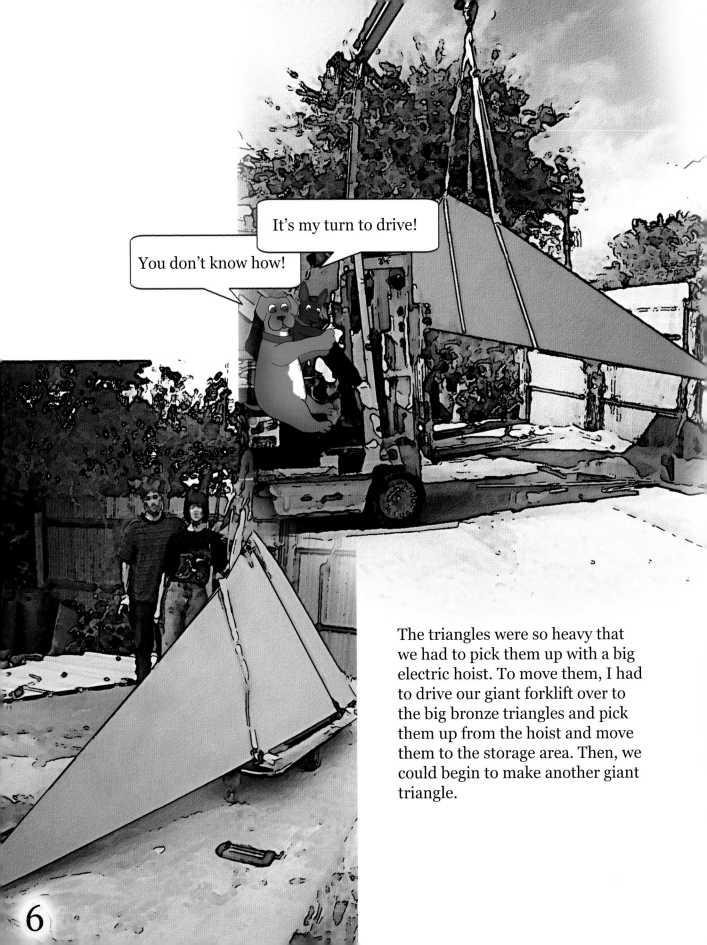

The triangles were so heavy that we had to pick them up with a big electric hoist. To move them, I had to drive our giant forklift over to the big bronze triangles and pick them up from the hoist and move them to the storage area. Then, we could begin to make another giant triangle.

This is a half cone

Working day after day, the time finally arrived when we finished welding together all 20 giant triangles. Next, we sat down and looked over our plan once again. Now that the 20 triangles were complete, we were ready to begin building 10 half cones. It was important that each of the 10 half cones were exactly the same. In order to make them the same, we had to build a jig. The jig was a big steel frame into which two giant triangles were placed to hold them straight and steady. This allowed us to weld them together, so that they were just the right shape every time.

We began welding the half cones during the month of August. Here in Austin, the month of August is very, very hot. In direct sunlight, our bronze plates soaked up so much heat, we could not touch them with our bare hands. Not only does the sun heat up the bronze plate, but when we weld the plates, they get even hotter. The welding process actually produces an electrical flame that is hot enough to melt the bronze plate. And since bronze conducts heat so quickly, the plate gets hot enough to fry eggs on it. It was good that we had special clothing to protect us from the heat!

As we built the half cones one by one, we placed them in the storage area to make room for the next ones. When we finished with the last half cone, we knew we were making good progress. We were now ready to proceed to the next important step—building the 5 full cones! When we started making the cones, our project began to grow taller and taller! This was different for us because now we had to start working on tall ladders.

To make a full cone, we lined up 2 half cones and welded them together. We found ourselves welding all day long, day after day. It's a good thing for me I love to weld, even though I have to concentrate really hard. It's very exciting for me to watch the two plates melt along with the welding rod and see the three different metals fuse together. Welding creates a very bright light and produces splatters of molten metal, so I had to wear a welding hood with a dark lens to protect my eyes and face. Sometimes after welding all day long, I would go to sleep at night and dream about welding all night long. When I awoke I felt like I was really tired from all that welding in my dreams! But after breakfast, I was always ready to put in another good day!

Many times we worked well into the night because we had to finish the work scheduled for that day. Then, each night before we went to bed, we talked about the work we did that day. While everything was still fresh in our minds, we wanted to review to make sure we had left nothing out.

It's going to be daylight soon.

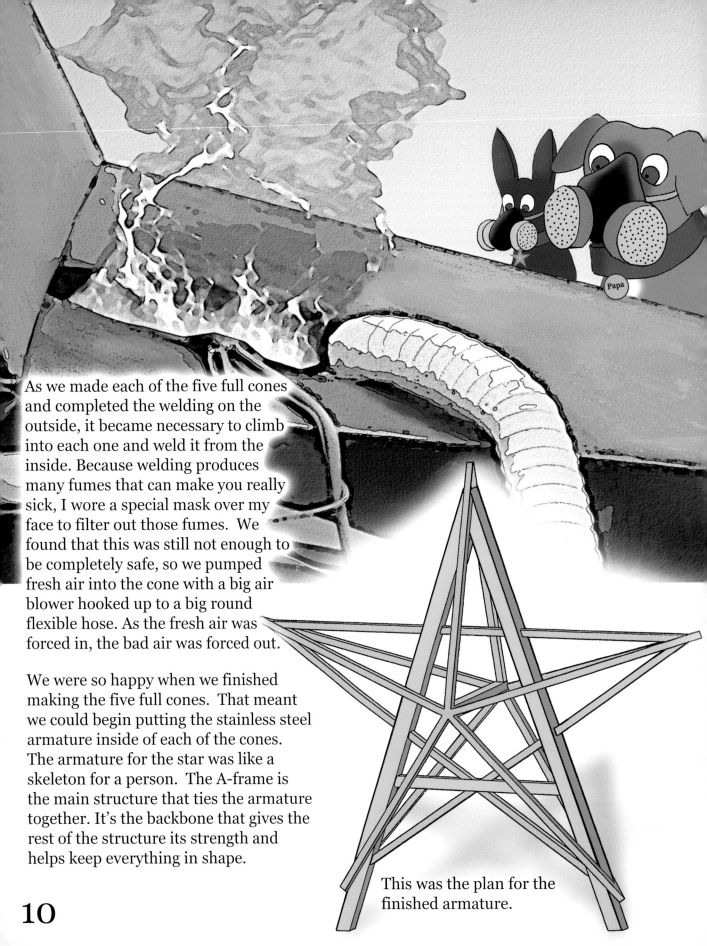

As we made each of the five full cones and completed the welding on the outside, it became necessary to climb into each one and weld it from the inside. Because welding produces many fumes that can make you really sick, I wore a special mask over my face to filter out those fumes. We found that this was still not enough to be completely safe, so we pumped fresh air into the cone with a big air blower hooked up to a big round flexible hose. As the fresh air was forced in, the bad air was forced out.

We were so happy when we finished making the five full cones. That meant we could begin putting the stainless steel armature inside of each of the cones. The armature for the star was like a skeleton for a person. The A-frame is the main structure that ties the armature together. It's the backbone that gives the rest of the structure its strength and helps keep everything in shape.

This was the plan for the finished armature.

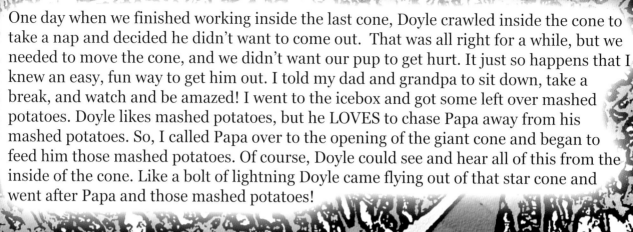

One day when we finished working inside the last cone, Doyle crawled inside the cone to take a nap and decided he didn't want to come out. That was all right for a while, but we needed to move the cone, and we didn't want our pup to get hurt. It just so happens that I knew an easy, fun way to get him out. I told my dad and grandpa to sit down, take a break, and watch and be amazed! I went to the icebox and got some left over mashed potatoes. Doyle likes mashed potatoes, but he LOVES to chase Papa away from his mashed potatoes. So, I called Papa over to the opening of the giant cone and began to feed him those mashed potatoes. Of course, Doyle could see and hear all of this from the inside of the cone. Like a bolt of lightning Doyle came flying out of that star cone and went after Papa and those mashed potatoes!

Mine, mine, mine!!!!

A-Frame

There's not enough room for another dog in this book.

Do you want me to bite him?

Papa

Now that all 5 cones were made, it was time to build the giant stainless steel main A-frame. The A-frame was nearly 40 feet tall and 23 feet wide. We built the giant A-frame while it was lying down on the ground. When it was finished we picked it up with two giant forklifts and put it inside two of the cones, which were already lying down and in position to receive the A-frame.

Cone

Cone

A-Frame

Jig

Star Legs

A-Frame

A-Frame

We called for a giant crane to come out and pick up the A-frame with its two star legs attached and stand it upright. Once it was in position, we bolted and braced it to the slab. The star now stood for the first time!

Bolt on the brace poles!

13

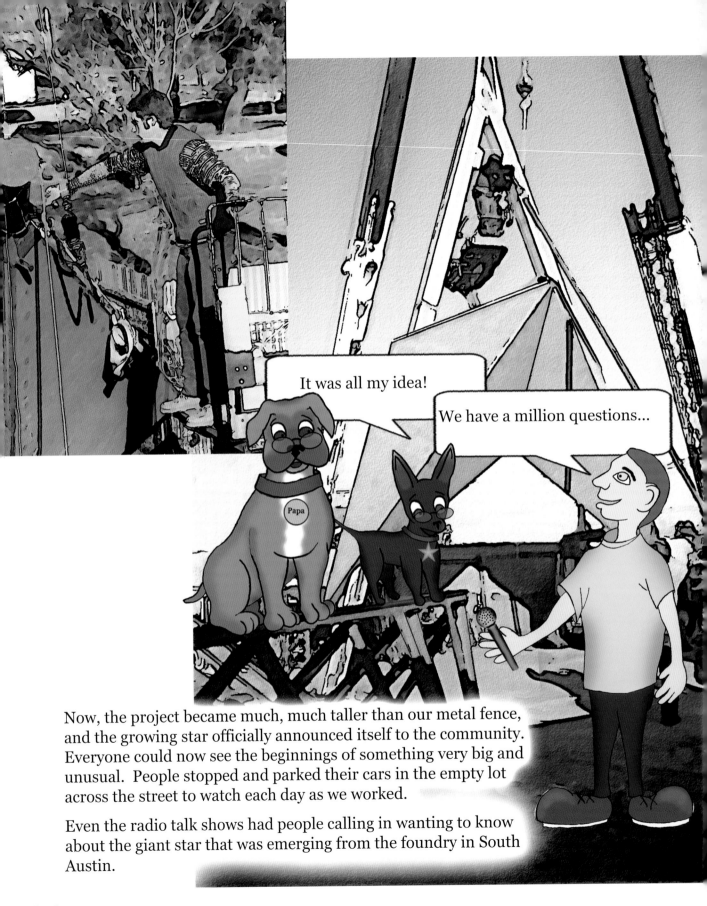

Now, the project became much, much taller than our metal fence, and the growing star officially announced itself to the community. Everyone could now see the beginnings of something very big and unusual. People stopped and parked their cars in the empty lot across the street to watch each day as we worked.

Even the radio talk shows had people calling in wanting to know about the giant star that was emerging from the foundry in South Austin.

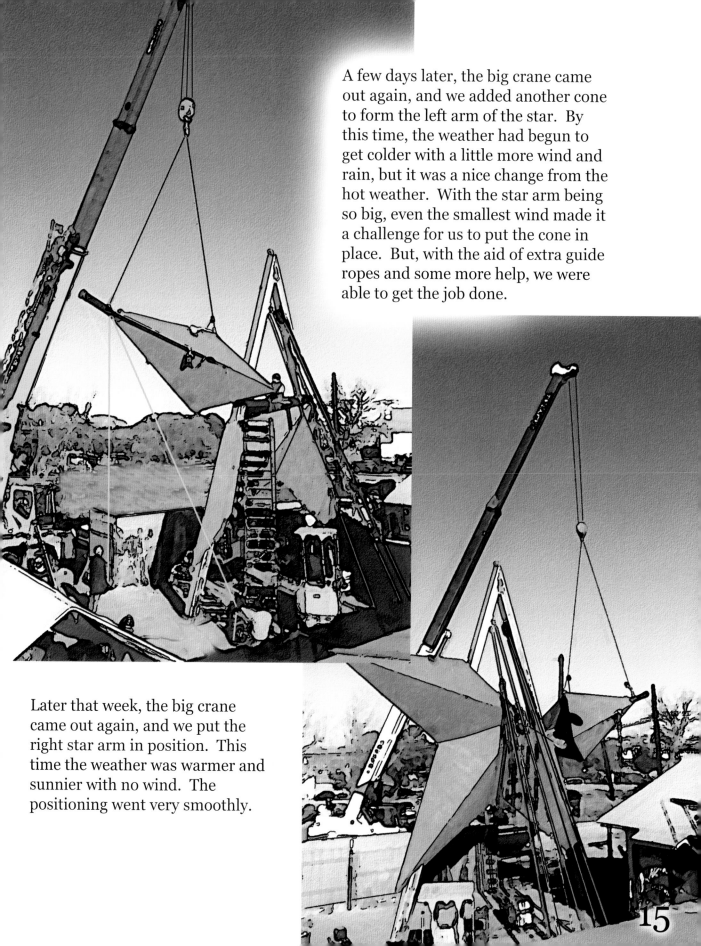

A few days later, the big crane came out again, and we added another cone to form the left arm of the star. By this time, the weather had begun to get colder with a little more wind and rain, but it was a nice change from the hot weather. With the star arm being so big, even the smallest wind made it a challenge for us to put the cone in place. But, with the aid of extra guide ropes and some more help, we were able to get the job done.

Later that week, the big crane came out again, and we put the right star arm in position. This time the weather was warmer and sunnier with no wind. The positioning went very smoothly.

Before we could put on the top star cone, we had about a week's worth of work on the inside of the star. We first built a floor in the center of the star's belly so that we would have a place to set our equipment. We also had water jugs, exhaust fans, and our walkie-talkies so we could communicate with the rest of the crew on the ground without having to crawl out of the star and lean over and yell down to them. Even though the weather was cool most of the time, we had days when the sun would shine brightly, making it really hot in the belly of the star. Because of this, we had to drink plenty of water and eat a lot of fruit and snacks between our regular meals just to keep our strength up. Because it was easier, we always ate our snacks while we worked high up in the belly of the star. Sometimes we even ate our lunch up in the star.

By the time supper came around, we were always ready to climb down out of the star and live at ground level for a while.

16

The "eagle" was a *metaphor* for the top cone...

After we completed all the necessary welding and made all our preparations, we were ready to put on the top cone. We had long-awaited that thrilling day! Our code word for the big event was "the eagle is landing." We joked around that the "eagle" had been waiting many months to make his landing, and the day had finally come.

That morning as the giant crane was setting up to install the top cone, many people stopped to watch the amazing event. Before long, the street and the sidewalks were crowded with people who came to watch the "eagle" land. The installation of the top cone went perfectly. It was a very calm day...good weather, no wind. The top cone came down over the A-frame just right and fit gently into its place.

The people cheered and clapped with joy because the "eagle" landed so perfectly. The biggest cheer of all, though, came from my family. We now had this very important step behind us.

17

Now that the top cone was in place, we had to spend about a week finishing up all the welding and details inside the star. So that we could get in and out of the star to do our work, we cut a small round hole in one of the arms.

Once inside, we needed lots of work lights because it was very dark inside. Except for the little ray of light that came through the manhole, it was pitch dark without the lights. I wore a headlamp on my forehead. That way when I needed extra light, I could have it and still have both of my hands free to work. We climbed in and out of the manhole for many days, finishing all of the work.

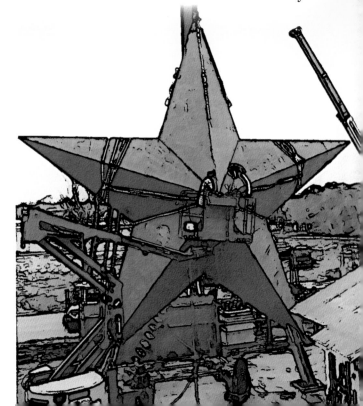

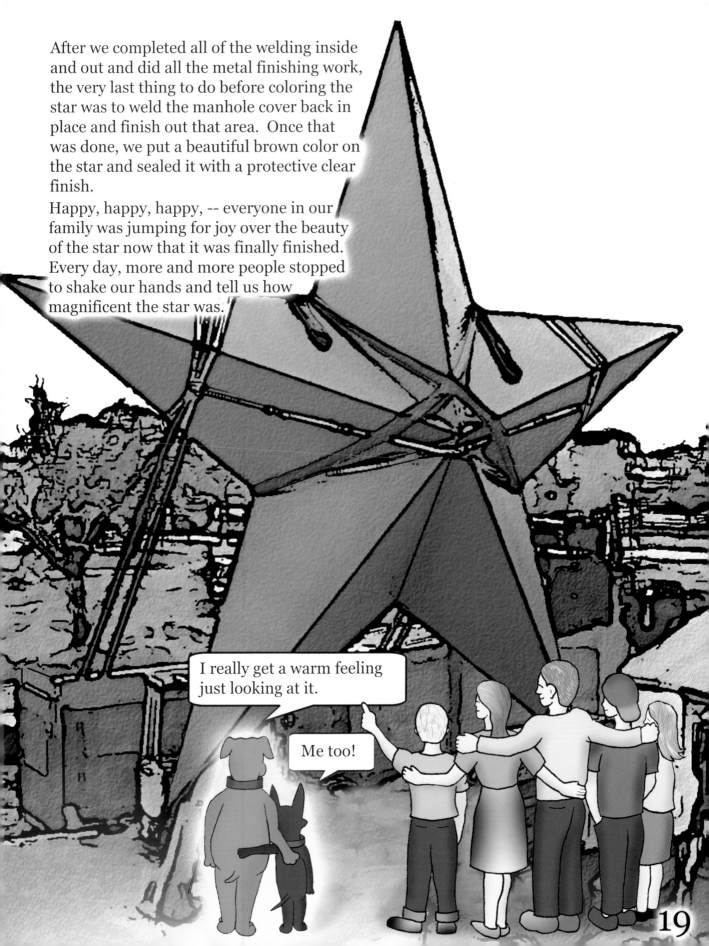

After we completed all of the welding inside and out and did all the metal finishing work, the very last thing to do before coloring the star was to weld the manhole cover back in place and finish out that area. Once that was done, we put a beautiful brown color on the star and sealed it with a protective clear finish.

Happy, happy, happy, -- everyone in our family was jumping for joy over the beauty of the star now that it was finally finished. Every day, more and more people stopped to shake our hands and tell us how magnificent the star was.

I really get a warm feeling just looking at it.

Me too!

Foam Cradle

Many people told us that they watched the star grow for months and months, and they wanted to meet and congratulate the people who built it. Every day more people would show up, and I would shake their hands and answer their questions about the star. After a few more weeks, we were ready to move the beautiful giant star from our shop to the brand new Bob Bullock Texas State History Museum here in Austin.

The building of the star was a sight to be seen, but the safe transportation of the star to the museum and then the installation at the museum was the most spectacular sight of all. My dad and I built a special foam cradle so the star could lay down. This huge cradle weighed 3,000 pounds and was over 10 feet wide and 10 feet long.

Foam Cradle

The day before the move, two giant cranes and a big 18-wheeler flat bed truck arrived, and we prepared to pick up the star and load it onto the truck. After a few hours, all of the equipment was in place and all the rigging straps were attached, so we were ready for the pick-up and loading of the star. We picked up the giant star and laid it down on its belly right into the big foam cradle. As it settled down into its nesting place we sighed with relief.

20

We loaded the star on a Saturday but didn't move it until Sunday morning, because the traffic would be lighter. Arrangements had been made with the city and the police department months in advance so that we could close down all of the lanes of all the streets where we would be traveling.

The police department did a wonderful job in directing all the traffic and giving us a full escort for the star. Moving it sure was exciting! The star was so wide that it barely fit around some of the turns we had to make. It's a good thing we had all the lanes of all the streets blocked off, because we needed all that space just to maneuver the star. It was quite a sight to see the star making its way slowly down the streets to its new home.

As the star passed by the State Capitol Building and then the Governor's Mansion, the Governor looked out of his window and smiled and waved as the giant star slowly passed by.

The most important person in the whole caravan was the driver of that great big 18-wheeler flat bed truck. Marvin had just the right touch on the gas and the brake pedals. He drove so smoothly and carefully that the star hardly even knew that it was being moved! Behind the star my mom drove one support truck with tools and equipment. My Uncle Bill drove the other support truck. Behind those trucks was a giant crane that followed us, just in case we couldn't make it around a turn with our extra wide load. The crane could pick up the entire rear end of the 18-wheeler and ease it around the corner to clear any poles or signs that might be in our way.

Behind the crane was a whole fleet of family vehicles. My grandmas and grandpas, aunts, uncles, and cousins were all there to celebrate the moving of the giant star to its important new home.

Even though the star was built only 5 miles away from the museum, it took about three hours to haul the star from our shop to the museum.

Finally, our long, slow, steady move was coming to an end as we approached the museum. The last few blocks of our journey, the streets were lined with people all wanting to see history in the making. When the star caravan pulled up in front of the museum, a huge crowd of people were anxiously awaiting their first glimpse of the giant "Star of Texas." A television station helicopter circled overhead so all the people in Austin could watch on TV. Newspaper reporters were there also.

Even families were there with cameras getting pictures of the great event! I was happy to see all the people who were responsible for the project growing from an idea to a 35 ft. tall, 20,000 lb. bronze star. As we unloaded the star with two giant cranes and set it into position, the awesome sight received whistles from the crowd. As my family and I stood back and looked at our great accomplishment, we hugged each other for a job well done. We all had a part in creating this wonderful monument, and we all did our jobs well! After almost one year of planning and discussion and work and dreams, it all came true. The star was standing before us at the brand new Bob Bullock Texas State History Museum in Austin, Texas, our State Capitol.

The brace poles fit into...

...these giant boxes filled with concrete.

24

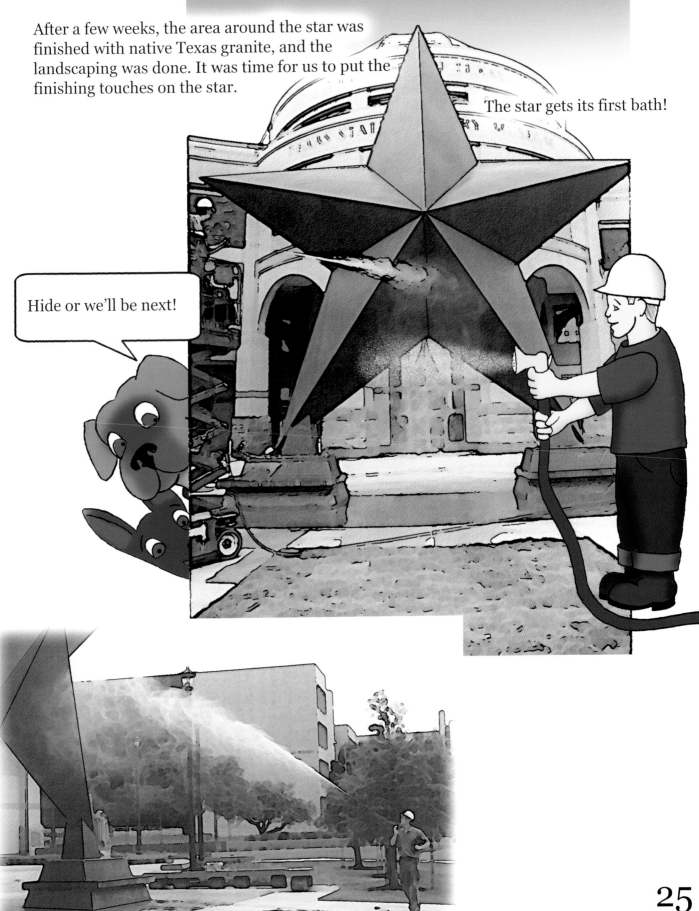

After a few weeks, the area around the star was finished with native Texas granite, and the landscaping was done. It was time for us to put the finishing touches on the star.

The star gets its first bath!

Hide or we'll be next!

25

Shortly after that, The President of the United States of America, George W. Bush, came to the new museum. As he stood under the star and spoke, the television cameras showed the event to the world. Mr. Bob Bullock would have been very proud to have been standing under the star that day. Yes, I was there with my family and we proudly watched and listened to the President speak. As I looked over at my dad, I noticed that he had a tear in his eye as he winked at me with a smile.

Well, it has been some time now since the star was born, but it seems just like yesterday to me. My family and I find ourselves visiting the star frequently. We look up at our big friend and have so many good memories. For now and forever, I will always have a warm, friendly feeling inside every time I think about my part in such a wonderful project. I know it's not really, but I will always see that big guy as MY STAR!

Our star now has a permanent home for all people to see for many, many generations to come. I know that someday when I have children and grandchildren, I will be taking them to see my star and telling them about our exciting adventure of the making of "The Star of Texas."

DID YOU KNOW?

The total weight of the star is 20,000 pounds.
> The bronze plate outer skin weighs 10,000 pounds.
> The internal stainless steel armature weighs 10,000 pounds.

Every morning when the sun comes out and begins to heat the star, the cool night air inside the star expands and a pressure builds up inside the star. To let this pressure escape we drilled small holes at the base of the star legs. (These holes are not visible now because they are hidden by the big granite blocks.) If you listen closely enough around the bench areas of the star legs, you may hear the star "breathe" for a couple of hours on sunny mornings.

The star stands on big concrete and steel support columns that go deep into the ground.

Even though the star is very large, 35 ft. tall, its angles cut through the wind, providing stability.

Our first step was to make a drawing. We then made a paper model, then a stiff cardboard model, then a wooden model, then a metal model, then an even larger wooden model, and finally the full size, monumental bronze star.

The Bob Bullock Texas State History Museum
Austin, Texas

29

NOTES FROM JOE: TO CHILDREN   (Maybe parents too!)

Do you have any questions about the making of "The Star of Texas?" I invite you to e-mail all of your questions to me at starbook@kassonscastings.com. I always enjoy talking about the star project, and I'll be waiting to answer your questions, so let me hear from you!

What is a sculptor?

A sculptor is a person who carves or models figures. Sculpture is what a sculptor produces. I have been sculpting since I was very young. I still have most of my sculpture from when I was younger, and it's fun for me to compare those to the sculpture I am now making.
I encourage you to begin to sculpt. Get some modeling clay and fashion and create anything that comes to mind. Get those hands busy and let your mind get into gear. Just begin at the beginning and develop your talents. You may be surprised at what you can create and where it could lead. Being a sculptor led me to acquiring some of the skills that I needed in the building of "The Star of Texas."

NOTES FROM JOE: TO PARENTS (Maybe children too!)

The Building of a Texas Icon: "THE STAR OF TEXAS" PRESENTATION

Kassons Castings has different programs in which we offer presentations to schools and organizations. Our "The Star of Texas" program shows the process of the construction, transporting, and installation of the 35 ft. tall bronze star standing in front of the Bob Bullock Texas State History Museum in Austin, Texas. This monumental bronze star weighs 20,000 lbs. and was constructed by Kassons Castings at their foundry in Austin. They then transported it in one piece and erected it on site at the museum. This project is documented and presented in a slide show of approximately one hour in length. Presented by John or Joe Kasson (usually both), this show is unforgettable.

This slide presentation is informative and entertaining, and connects with every age level. The topic and manner in which it is presented captures the attention of children as well as adults.

This experience successfully accomplishes the following:

*Introduces the audience to practical, real world applications of the academics taught in school settings.
*Provides a close-up look at a labor intensive hands-on project with some of the main ingredients being enthusiasm, creativity, and problem solving.
*Exposes the audience to the creation of a monumental project through the eyes of its creators-- three generations of the same family constructing a Texas icon.
*Allows the audience to be a part of the making of "The Star of Texas" through seeing and becoming aware of the processes and techniques involved in the making of this significant, historical Texas monument.
*Creates an interest and awareness in the various aspects of sculpture and its interaction with society.
*Demonstrates that hard work and dedication can be fun and funny!

Check out our website at www.kassonscastings.com or
contact us at starbook@kassonscastings.com to inquire about the presentations.

30